The Essential Gorter - Volume 2

Selected Poems

Herman Gorter

Selected Poems

Translated by Lloyd Haft

ISBN 978-90-831336-52

Introduction and English translation : © 2021 Lloyd Haft. First edition.

Selected Poems is Volume 2 of *The Essential Gorter* by Arimei Books.
Also read Volume 1 : *May, an epic poem about youth.*

Cover illustration & design : © 2021 Eva Polakovičová (evapola.com).
Published by Arimei Books.
www.ArimeiBooks.com

Contents

Foreword

The Netherlands has not done a good job of preserving its literary heritage: poets from bygone eras tend to drift quickly into oblivion. But Herman Gorter (1864-1927) is a prominent exception; some of his works are still widely read and admired. Aside from the epic *May* (1889), it is especially his lyric verse – a genre that he continued to pursue throughout his stormy life – that is popular. Less well known, for no good reason, is the impressive epic *Pan* (two versions, 1912 and 1916), which sings the heroic struggle of the labor movement.

Gorter, a specialist in classical languages who wrote his Ph.D. thesis on the metaphors of Aeschylus, is renowned for his sensual language and subtle rhythmic effects. Since Gorter distorts the Dutch language and adjusts it to what he wants to say, sometimes using words that can't be found in any dictionary, translating his poetry demands the utmost from the translator.

May has been translated into German, French, Frisian, Russian, and (recently) English, but a really extensive translation of his other works into a world language did not yet exist.

The sinologist and poet Lloyd Haft (1946), whose earlier work includes a rewriting of the Psalms (2003), has had the courage to translate a wide selection of Gorter's work into English. In Haft's version, Gorter sounds the way he should sound: musical and sensitive, at times groping, at other times jubilant, always sure of himself and amazing. No other Dutch poet's work is as exciting as Gorter's, so

much so that you sometimes downright fall in love with it.
For readers of English it will be a feast to be able to make
his acquaintance via this translation.

Piet Gerbrandy

Introduction

Herman Gorter (1864-1927) is one of the all-time great Dutch poets. Most Netherlanders, even if they seldom or never read poetry, are familiar with Gorter's often-quoted line *Een nieuwe lente en een nieuw geluid*, literally 'A new springtime and a new sound.' They may or may not know that this is the opening line of *May* (Mei, 1899), a long story poem with which Gorter instantly became famous when he was only twenty-four. An epic of youth and passion against a background of vibrant nature imagery, *May* is written in traditional rhymed couplets. Thematically as well as in form, at times it shows influence of Keats' *Endymion* or of the drama and diction of Old Norse mythology. In subsequent books, starting with *Verses* (Verzen, 1890), Gorter wrote in a radically new style which combined experimentally intense lyricism with a freewheeling approach to language. Changing the spelling or even the sound of words to make them rhyme, inventing his own words, using words in an archaic or dialect sense – all these devices went into Gorter's own brand of Dutch, making it a rich but challenging brew for reader and translator alike. Tastes differ; Gorter's linguistic fireworks seem brash to some readers, brilliant to others. Even highly educated Dutch speakers are not always sure just what a given phrase means, or which of its alternative possibilities is most likely to apply.

As Gorter's career evolved, the creative oddity of his language was one thing which alienated a certain proportion of readers; another was his emerging ultra-Leftist political stance. Gorter believed that every human being is motivated by three fundamental drives: self-preservation or self-love, the sex instinct or love for the opposite sex, and the communal instinct or love for the community. This last factor he personally identified, to the dismay of many readers, with the ideals of socialism and communism. Difficult as it might seem to see these three forms of love simultaneously embodied in an idealized female 'other' who could be addressed in poetry, Gorter tried to do so.

When Gorter first broke into prominence with *May* in the late 1880s, he was associated with the literary movement called in Dutch the *Tachtigers*, literally the Eightiers. Rebelling against the stodgy, moralistic writings of many Dutch writers of their day, the Eightiers strove for a poetry of hyper-individualistic emotional expression. Their ideals were more aesthetic than social. When *May* came out in early 1889, it was immediately hailed as a pinnacle of the new movement.

By autumn of the following year, when Gorter's *Verses* appeared, it was clear that he had undergone a transformation. No longer treading in the recognizable footsteps of his Dutch or English Romantic forebears, he was now writing literally 'verses' in which it seemed every new moment of experience was autonomous, demanding its own spontaneous configuration of sound and image. These poems were unlike anything in the tradition. They seemed to call for an ongoing celebration of the cutting edge of consciousness. *Verses* has been called 'the Sergeant Pepper of Dutch poetry,' and the effect on many, especially young readers must indeed have been almost psychedelic. The eminent writer Lodewijk van Deyssel, reviewing the poems in the Eightiers' magazine *De nieuwe gids*, wrote that Gorter had 'seen behind the perceptible into timelessness... There is no adjective for it. It reaches the ultimate boundary of what is thinkable.' In what became a standard scholarly study of the Eightiers (1934), Garmt Stuiveling praised the *Verses* for their 'comprehensiveness of feeling' and 'visionary lucidity.' In a later article, Victor van Vriesland said Gorter had realized 'the utmost psychic possibilities of Dutch words.'

But *Verses*, too, for Gorter was but one stage in an ongoing development. He could not long remain satisfied with a kind of writing that seemed unconcerned with larger social issues. During the 1890s he grew increasingly critical of an individualist focus in the arts. In a seemingly retrograde move, he wrote sonnets – though, typically for him, they were anti-traditional in both rhythm and vocabulary – and in 1897 he came out with a frequently-quoted critique of the Eightiers movement. In the same year he began studying Karl Marx.

By the early twentieth century Gorter was increasingly focused on social and socialist ideals. In 1909 he joined the Social Democratic Party, which would later become the Communist Party of the Netherlands. He continued writing poetry but was also taken up with turbulent personal affairs. Two young women who had come to him for private lessons in classics eventually became his lovers. He kept each secret from the other and they did not meet until both attended his funeral in 1927. One of them, Jenne Clinge Doorenbos (1887-1973), became the real-life muse of his many love lyrics; she was also a very active sounding board in Gorter's poetry writing and editing. Eventually she was also co-editor (with Garmt Stuiveling) of the eight-volume set of his *Collected Works* (Verzamelde werken, 1948-1952).

In 1912, Gorter again turned to writing an epic. This time it was *Pan,* in which Pan, as god of nature, falls in love with a 'golden girl' who is the Spirit of the New Humanity. Prophetically, it described a coming great war to be followed by world revolution. A much expanded version was published in 1916.

True to his independence of mind, in *Pan* Gorter reversed the genders traditionally associated with physical and spiritual life. In *Pan,* the representative of earthly instinct is the male god Pan; it is the woman or 'maiden' who personifies the spirit. Their story is a long one, occupying some 400 pages as published in the *Collected Works.* But the scenic decors of their love (and lovemaking) include some of Gorter's most impressive nature poetry. One almost wonders how Gorter found time to write long narrative poems like *May* and *Pan;* he would seem to have needed countless hours of his life just to observe and remember nature as minutely as he did. How a rainstorm develops, beginning with faint 'silken' inklings, continuing through a heavier phase of pounding 'diamonds,' then 'softening its streaming' as clouds of fragrance arise, until finally 'the pliant rain settles into the forest' – this we find noted in passing as if it were an effortlessly sketched backdrop. Gorter's descriptions are not just rhetorical pile-ups of words found in dictionaries. We feel that he really has seen the 'shone-through vague rough bigness' of trees in a forest, the ocean waves 'falling over the top and forward...crashing full bouldering swaying striped dark-faceted water.' Perhaps it is no wonder that Gorter

Selected Poems

identified with Pan, god of nature, considering that nature is the setting and the inspiration of so much of his poetry.

In most introductions to Gorter's life and work, *Pan* is mentioned as an important work, perhaps even his only notable effort after *May* and *Verses*. Much less attention is paid to the very impressive long lyric sequence, posthumously published, called *Lyrics* (Liedjes, literally 'little songs,' 1930). Gorter worked on these poems from 1910 to 1924 – partly at least in the same period that he was working on *Pan*. Certain passages from *Pan* show up in *Lyrics* as well. An example is the following poem from *Pan*, addressed ostensibly to the Spirit:

> O Golden Spirit
> of Freedom,
> I'm thrusting higher now,
> thrusting into ever brighter, whiter, golder
> Joy,
> into your golden Body.
>
> O Chalice
> heaven-seeming!
> Into your deep teeming
> may all someday rise –
>
> Goal!
> that the drift eternal
> hot and cool
> is driving to.
>
> Longing
> ever greater
> as the womb climbs
> higher above it.

Womb,
depth without end,
ever farther
as the longing lengthens.

Joy. Woman. Humanity.
Longing that never ends
O! because the rising of humanity
is nowhere bounded.

In *Lyrics*, the first strophe appears as a separate poem, the second is deleted, and the third through sixth are a continuous sequence of separate poems.

In the starkly minimalized stage settings of *Lyrics*, the imagery becomes almost alchemical. Rather than a description, it is a transmutation of nature. The fire and water elements originally seen in sun and sea reappear as interacting energies:

My Beloved
as water pure
came into the fire
of love.

...

...

Deep into the fount
the sun finally fell.
And the fount
rose to heaven.

Lyrics is more loosely structured than *Pan*; it does not form a narrative but is like a slide show of mini-episodes. It is like an etherealized, more private version of *Pan*, still set against the background of a longed-for 'new humankind' represented by a woman, but with a crucial change – the male protagonist of the erotic scenes is usually no longer the god Pan but 'I.' *Lyrics* represents Gorter's ultimate effort to combine the love for a woman with love for humanity as he conceived it within his communist political ideals. Here, the beautiful 'Lady' or 'Maiden' stands both for herself and for the 'new humankind' that Gorter hoped the Revolution would bring into being. In the coda-like fourth section of Book Three, after the initially despondent tone of 'The Defeat of the Revolution,' Gorter comes back to reassert his concept of the three basic loves. In a magnificent sequence of three similarly worded sonnets, he again sees visions of the beloved woman, himself, and humanity against a heavenly background.

Gorter perhaps did not see fit to, in any event did not, publish the *Lyrics* sequence during his lifetime. He had it privately printed in three copies, one for himself and one for each of his two lovers. It was published for all the world to see in 1930, three years after Gorter's decease.

Gorter is not 'difficult' to translate; he is impossible... unless the translation is a labor of both love and luck and can convey to the reader at least some glint of the impulse which inspired the original poems. To begin with, the words on the page. How to translate a language (Dutch) in which one and the same word (*schoot*) can mean 'lap,' 'bosom,' or 'womb'? And this in poems by a man who was straining to achieve a join between the beauty of a woman's anatomy and the beauty of her...ah yes, her what? considering that the same word (*geest*) can mean 'mind' but also 'spirit.' Are we to admire her wise thoughts (mind), or her passionate ideals and hopes (spirit)? Examples of both can be found in the poems.

Again, *leest* often suggests the 'form' or 'figure' of a person's body rather than the body as such, yet in a poem on Spinoza's philosophy, Gorter unmistakably uses the rhyme-pair *geest* and *leest* to refer to the opposing poles of 'spirit' and 'body.' In the first strophe of the poem from *Pan* which I have translated above, I read them to be used in the same senses.

So far I have only mentioned the 'legitimate' or 'dictionary' meanings of words. But Gorter is the supreme player on words, their sounds, their possible and perhaps-barely-possible associations. In a short poem from *Verses*,

> Her eyes glimmering chalices,
> her hand silent red,
> her body a calyx
> welling from her womb.

in the first line of the original, the 'chalices' are *kelken*, plural, with the normal plural suffix *-en*. In the third line, the 'calyx' in the original is *kelke*, a word you will not find in any dictionary. No matter, obviously it is *kelk* with an extra *-e* to give it an added syllable and make it rhyme with *kelken*. The translation is problematical. *Kelk* can mean 'chalice' but also 'calyx.' Is her 'body' a veritable flower? Very plausible. But in the original it is described as *wèlle*, again a non-existent word, which commentators have taken

Selected Poems

to mean 'welling up.' So, is a *wèlle kelke uit haren schoot* a 'chalice, welling from her womb' or a 'calyx, stemming from her womb'? Probably for Gorter it was both, and for the imaginative reader it can be both. But we have to come out with a single translation. I have chosen for the calyx, calling it 'welling' to keep it somewhat chalice-like.

The present book is a companion volume to M. Kruijff's superb translation of Gorter's epic *May*. The poems I have chosen to translate are:

(1) twenty-two poems from *Verses* (1890);
(2) fifteen other short, intense poems from later collections;
(3) nine selected lyrical passages from *Pan* (1916); and
(4) my abridged but substantial version of *Lyrics* (1930), not including all the poems but maintaining the order and overall structure of the original.

The four sections of my book correspond to the main successive stages in Gorter's career after his initial breakthrough with *May* in 1889. concluding with *Lyrics* (1930). Within each section the order of the poems, except in *Lyrics*, is of no particular significance but follows the order in the *Collected Works*. Gorter himself does not seem to have intended the original *Verses* as a structured sequence: in a later republication he changed the order and deleted many of the poems. The poem I translate on page 25 originally appeared in *Verses* as three separate poems; in later editions they were always combined into one, as in my translation.

Lyrics has never before appeared in English. My version comprises about sixty percent of the original. It is in the interest of maintaining musicality and focus that I have chosen to omit some of the poems that seemed to me ineffectively repetitious, or which I could not get to sound plausible in translation. Stuiveling included a radically short selection from *Lyrics* (about one-sixth of the whole) in the selected volume of Gorter's poems which he edited in 1956. That book has been reprinted many times and is a standard introduction to Gorter. My selection is not only much longer than Stuiveling's but includes some of the more explicitly political poems like the sonnets to Karl Liebknecht and Rosa Luxemburg. But like Stuiveling and like another major Gorter anthologist, J. C. Brandt Corstius whose selection came out in 1946, I could not get myself to include the hero-worshipping sonnet to Lenin.

My translations do not rigidly reproduce the rhyme-schemes of the originals – that would have imposed a too crippling limitation on the available choice of words – but they do, I think, fairly represent the overall sound and texture of Gorter's verse.

For the reader who wishes to consult the Dutch originals, it is easy to access online, and to download free of charge, the texts as they are included in Gorter's *Collected Works*. In the appendix, together with a brief pointer to the relevant links, I list the volume and page in the *Collected Works* where each translated poem begins.

On the completion of this book which I first began to envision some four decades ago, I wish to thank Jan Bouts for introducing me to *Lyrics*, Jan Kuijper for sharing his knowledge of Gorter's vocabulary and poetics, Henk van der Ent for astute comments on difficult passages, and Agnès van Rees for help with nuances in translation.

Lloyd Haft
August 2021

Selected Poems

From *Verses* (1890)

When times were leaf-still, long gone by,
born she was, in autumn hush a bloom
in bleak lightweepings standing pale light –
the clouds cloak her in rains.

Pale she stood her light amidst all drear,
keeping light eyes, blonde hair spreading near her,
tears at many an hour, white of hands –
a poor light girl light-famished.

Bring upon her color of bloomglow,
your blood-red, o new season that is now.

WE BEINGS OF SILVER, LIGHTS OF MIST, GROWTHS
neighboring each other uncertain, wanted light:
in mists of dark our great needs
foreign in shimmering mist, for light –
tender beginning and smiling shine,
lightly rising, shunning to fade,
laughing as sure, shining with joylight,
waving and fleeting, looking back in flight,
willows of light, ribbons of light, whitish silver
waterish light, luring light, scythes of shivering light,
sheaths and bayonets of light – army of light.

Our flesh blooming with light, gorging on light,
hearts swelling with light, breaking light,
eyes gossamer light, crystal crowns of light.

You are a white and silent shining snow,
you are a shivering sea of shining sea.

You are a lilymaiden shimmerwhite,
you are a palehood fluttering wide.

You are the open, the white, the willing,
the waiting beaming flaming quivering light.

THE SILENT ROAD
the moonnightlighted road –

the trees
the trees so silently grown old –
the water
contented water stretched out calm.

And far behind, the sunken heaven
crawling with stars.

PALLOR OF GREY,
pitter of rain –
wet are the roofs, the wind
sings its meager lay.

The slow human ruckus
goes on. They call it work:
that sober daily going
without ever knowing.

O, for a lass to bloom this way
in brightish pale,
a lilyhood and bleary
unto me, the warm, the weary.

A CHILD EVER LONGING
as a great bloom's heart, hanging
open, born that way
in the dawning day.

I SAW YOU THEN –
and there was much of light,
the room was a bloom, tight
bud now shining out and open,
buzzed by rings of light.

Nothing that I thought or said.
You looked at me and all my head
came open windblown wide
like burning summer-open over wide, wide land
in country wide and worldly-open –
so, once, was I
within that chamber red and golden-lined
by gas-gold flamelight flown on rowing flapping
wings already beating away
in the fragile air
the trembling air
that flees us as we go –
hear hear, o I hear it,
your tender drythroat voice above me
speaking, speaking lower near me,
I scented your tender flesh,
your shining out, your silent living flesh –
and I was bursting with your eyeing
tingling naked eyeing
from that silent moving gaze,
that trembling and that moving
of your hands your head your feet

as even now it does to me.
If only I could find
that fleet outflowing galaxy,
the river of words: that I could say
this all before I die away
in floating through my life.
But o, the fair, the tingling tint
within the giant doors of light
that is sunsummer's –
all the light's belightedness,
the high and holy eucharist
of all the days
and goldlight evenshine
in the reddened room, that are the things
she was within,
body diaphanous
as glass and lightful – o pray be
pronounced together ever, in me
who saw her once and only
in your red and white and golden day.

Now let me go on trembling,
let me quiver on away
in words, so henceforth not a thing there is
but her belightedness.

SHADOWS WALK THE CHAMBERS OF HER EYES,
slow dreamrobes slow to depart,
opal shadows round her neck encoiffed.

And light blue and red tints lining
the pale-veiled sleeves of lace,
the conch lying open on her breast creamy –
and slowly out of the dark and grief of dusk
high-arched hills arise
as when the hills toward evening can be seen,
and slowly the high breast and the belly
sink again in lifeless sinkings
while smoky breath again departs the hearth
in swirls of wind.

I WISH YOU WERE THE AIR
so I could breathe you
and see you high in light
and interweave you –

where are your arms and hands?
and those white and more than splendid lands,
your shoulders and your shining breast?
I hunger and I thirst.

THESE ARE THE PALE, THE BLEAKLIT WEEKS –
I see the people moving, sticking
their shabby heads into mum daylight,
each a solitary sight.

I hear them speaking to each other
words that pale and fall far short
and then they're gone again
and it's a lonely road.

My head is empty and my mouth is dry,
my eyes burning skyward;
cold and dusty white
is all this light I'm in.

My head's between my hands that sense
each other: warm walls of flesh;
my legs are tired through and through
from the living that is what I'm doing.

From Verses (1890)

HER EYES GLIMMERING CHALICES,
her hand silent red,
her body a calyx
welling from her womb.

In the silence of the city
she came, her skirt rustled,
she held her white hands silent,
I listened.

THE RAY-PARADING DAY,
earthwide skyday,
spring in never-seen
light, blue muslin
whitish brilliance above –
alone the single eye of sungold.

And in the room
calm glory, pearly light,
not a single ray of sun.

FAR OFF I SAW BRIGHT WATERS,
nearby was gentle splashing
of a voice I know;
around it all was silence
that I heard above the slender flow
of words from in her gentle speaking.
All was silent but the voice's splash
with waters shining bright behind,
and I heard wordlets moving
crystal-clear through glassy silence.

My pale tinglepure
my white cuddlefine
with high from on high the whirling
of your hands seeming
the wingwave of birds,
the circling round of windmill sails,
feathering so finely through the air
my ear hears no sound
and your cheeks gliding close
and your lips barely open
motionless in red –
till suddenly from within them fled
a cool round wordspeech,
words cool as round hands
laying themselves in mine,
full, blooded, bloomfine –
it came and touched me,
up against my ears
coolblown, awn-fine,
no sooner red than gone.

THERE WAS MUCH YELLOW OAKENGOLDEN
light risen and grown in green, so much
shuddering of bluegolden
quaking white, for an instant grey
when the eye was hurt
by sunny piercing pain.

Mirror was the air as if
I walked now everywhere,
swollen hot as if I now
were myriad.

THERE WAS SNOW ON THAT MOSS,
she lay upon it loosened,
her lips wet and open,
eyes wet and open.

Her hand tapped the ground,
unhurried fingerwhite,
her shoulders shaping round
in blue on snowwhite.

The eyes beneath me
pearly oval –
she seemed a part of me
from me gone stray.

OUT ON THE STREET NOW SHINING SUN,
out on the street a human cry,
clatter of rattling carts
in the dozing distance.

The lampgold-bright allurement
of light enchambered, the reddish
constellation of book-backs –
what's there comes dreaming wakefully
behind the settled lineaments
of gleaming furnishings.

THE LAMP SHINES, THE ROOM IS OPEN –
outside, I hear the wind walking.
The leaves, the flapping leaves,
the springflapping leaves – the nightflapping leaves,
green and black and limp –
their wet lips, limp handclap –
hear it blowing up and all the ways away,
and there they come again –
that gentle-weaponed skirmish in the dark,
banging on each other
hear them ranting far away,
the night is fully open
as a floodgate –
grazing my hand a cool kiss, a stroking –
light as if in smoke enshone,
almost as if to go to sleep
in light's seeming, clingleafed up and down.

ALWAYS THAT METAL RUSTLING OF THE METAL-BEAMING SEA
and the wild-lighted crashing, cruel weight of waves,
the flashing biting fine-rayed infinite,
the overwidespread flooding walling in,
and yet that rolling in, full wet blue,
deep waterful of spraying drift,
fine to the eye, eye-quenching dawn of water
with over it straight-on streamers of wind –
that ladies' cheeks go by in, blooming close
in parasolsilver, fine-dangled hands
gemlike in eyeshine.

THE SEA BEYOND A GREY, SILVERISH, RAINISH, LEAFERY
spread in a circle of clouds –
here, o here fragile quiet green
widened into the wide,
my head, o my head in the weak and easeful air –
my eyes so cool, so rained for the air,
my hands so warmish hanging down –
o in a balmy sad surround by the going
cliffish wave-astraying sea
I held my head in hands –
but sprayish the glitterish rustling, thunderwhisper,
gurgling murmur, tongueflash leaking –
the blood in my hand is dry –
now shadow, seaful sea-ish where I see it.

THE WAVES AND THEIR FALLING OVER THE TOP AND FORWARD
with their flaunting so charming so silly so forgotten
ever and always wanting to be above all –
and then the sinking together, no longer wishing to be
the whole but deep under others, they sink expiring
with their dully loyal water-human eyes,
each mumbling to other, standing under another
all of them low and low and now no one higher –
thundering up they go to the preening high and lonely
sky that lights the world –
crashing full bouldering swaying striped dark-faceted water,
fullgreen whitefoam breasting foam-dribbling water,
water still but turning to light, yet lightly,
yet staring lovely lonely, the mute godworldly light
of heaven – and here the lowly greenfondling grass
laid to the wind, eyeing away, bending back
to the trees in the clumped quiet ground.

Other short poems

Deepest pain wrings onto the heart
figures of love clear
and comely as the darkness
on a shell, ivory-pure.

LIKE THE COOL CORRIDORS
of an empty house, full
of a gleam, a soft
whisper along the walls
of an absence –
so my soul is full
of your presence.

THE GREY SKIES HUNGER
as plunging clouds lengthen
and the twigtrees draw back
into their meager leanings,
shaped up once from ground, now
fading into horizon.
Torn fields lie
between hedges with blackening eyes.
The last of the skywhite lingers, evening
hungers down the road.

HINTS OF SUN, COMING
almost to glitter
on the glassy pane's
summerpitterpatter:

the muffled rasp
of the sparrows' sound – even that
the white ripe light's
found in.

IN A SELFFORGOTTEN CORNER
of the scent of oaks, sitting far and small before
the major stage, the vaster mass of trees –
see how their interplaying dreams them
on and outward, into skies of silver –
first they're trees, then they're the beginnings
of silver air, and others lying farther
and higher, more together, out we-wider.
As set-in-motion evening comes:
green trees mutely wait, standing ready.

While the wind shone and the bee buzzed:
a silent moment of happiness found.
Then the air came open and I saw
clearly the trees standing into day
in their shone-through vague rough bigness,
and the glorious land of clouds, vague and nudged
aside by other greys. The sun shone,
blazed out, became immensities.
My ears were filled with feeling so at ease
I walked among all things, from all things freed.

THE SUN, THE SUN IN WHITE FIRE;
the forests with their gentle tarry stare
bend low now, forgetting green
for somber death in the raging
of the fires:
the burning of the hours
of afternoon.

THE OPEN AND SO CLEAR EARTH-LIFE,
and in it stands my eye-life,
warm breath leaving my lips,
ears ringing in the not-yet-understood.
The room hangs high, and at the window
the silent table stands under the fray
of curtains – outside, the silent land-lay
of things perceptible along the roads.
The sky is far, very far,
hurting it's so far –
as the eyes retrace their evident lost way.

THE GRASS HAS STARTED IN
on night: the calm-sunned garden,
sky still unthinking,
light so unbroken.

Trees white as buckwheat
hang in quiet beauty
but the loose chestnut leaves
are skittish, starting to feel
the weight of the wind.

The Mistrain Comes Telling
its tales athwart the green hymns of spruces
while they stand shrugging their shoulders
at how little tangles matter.
Sorrow prevails in the corners of the forests:
drab indifferent moldy mists
moving over the skewing trees
that waving break up skyward.

STAGGERSTEPPING THROUGH THE STAGGERSTEPPING WIND
and pounding rain – warm childhood
showed itself again.
Rushings in my ears, I felt
and saw ongoing the rainy days of old
and me ongoing. Scarce-budded was the spring
but full of rain. Memory was open
as day. A moment was a high beat
of the heart. And memory
showed itself a lasting consecration.

A WOMAN LIKE THE WORLD, HER FACE A BLANK
with laughter, thick and round, loose-
armed – high stiff breasts that stay beside her
like high hills lying athirst
in the roaming light – fixed high swellings
you can stay lying beside, telling
stories to yourself in the chirping, bird-slurped
light of awakening.

STORMY ARE THE WHITE TURBULENCES
of evening, and my face is turning
wallward – my heart mutely learning
to be as an eye among mute flatnesses.

It's living raw, and full of depths
beyond accounting, it eats me, consumes my eyes,
growing like a tree, like cabbage multiplying
in my tender loose flesh limbs.

I think my heart will someday still
be yonder among the rains that water it,
the leaves surrounding, climbing high
and facing it in a gigantic growth.

A life's becoming evident through me,
my waiting eyes burn so abundantly.

WHEN YOU LIE BENEATH ME AND WE'RE HUSHED
in fire, your face is white with love as it
beholds me, and your eyes are full of tears.
You never thought there could be such a thing
on earth, your eyes like two lakes filling
from the wellsprings in your heart.
The way we're strung together
your eyes trace two lines up and into mine.
I never thought that such things were, on earth.
And we both, thinking all such in our brains,
are strung together, arms sheltering heads,
we're as the land and ocean strung together
or the mountain and its valley, one together.

The way the ocean wafts a song landward
let me, with a face white with passion,
resound for you forever
with the thankfulness that's mine.

O LOVE, IT IS AS IF ALL COLORS,
now you're lying under me,
go forth in silence from your face
to paint the world.
It is as if your face becomes
the all of All, your colors flowing
through the atmosphere. Your face:
it colors all, it is the all.
As if in your face I'm seeing all
of life, all of nature's yielding,
risen, here cohering
in a single wave: your face. It is
her body's crown that lies here unresisting.

O let me say in silence that I love you,
and prove to you in silence that I love you:
I fill you with my all, feel your inward,
how yielding it is, how intimate, how soft.
In the high-as-heaven of the highest joy,
into the high-as-heaven, the ideal –
in I thrust through you. A dome of joy
comes open: into it through you I rise.

From *Pan* (1916)

A new love is arising in my heart
great and silent.
Like a flower rising from its stem and calyx
it rushed up through my heart, cleaving
a way its own, and naked gave
itself unto my eyes: this love was new.

And now I see my new love,
unraveled from the crystal of my eyes:
how through the all of All
she goes, like a Being hovering above
to whom I softly cry:
'Who art Thou, my love?'

She says, in a voice clear as crystal,
standing there upright in gold:
'I am the love
that rose up from your breast:
Love for the all of All.'

And shining as the Love that's nowhere bounded
softly my bright Love walked on,
on to Humanity.

SHE IS THE NEW LOVE.
She is the Sun
sprung from the Source
of Humanity.

'OUT OF THE ABYSS THE DARK BLUE COLORS OF THE PAST
flash like a dark blue dale of daffodils
and Its trumpet call resounds in the light of love
through the lightning of today.

And I, dark Pan with that dark Music and All-Love,
dance gloriously the dark ebb
of the golden Past, holding in my arms
the limbs of the Spirit of Future Music.

Piercing deep, her golden eyes of daydawning
fix me while I lead her in the dance;
out of the golden deeps of those arching daysprings
streams into me a filling, welling glory.

And full as I am, I can hardly walk
but only dance. Her burning golden gaze,
the love upon her in fine gold lightning
is nothing but the light of joyful dance.'

'Sparkling gold, from far above shine endless spirit precincts
like bournless fields of daffodils,
of the waiting future spirits of humanity, that waited
while I hastened toward dark Pan.

From Pan (1916)   65

All in gold I plunge as if an arrow
onto your heart, Pan, your dark luscious heart.
You'll offer up your bloom and blood for me;
my gold is the fulfillment of your dark.

Always you have craved our golden oneness;
nothing in your mighty all-inclusion
was strong as this drive, this dark fire,
o dance with me, God of dark Nature.'

O GOLDEN SPIRIT
of Freedom,
I'm thrusting higher now,
thrusting into ever brighter, whiter, golder
Joy,
into your golden Body.

O Chalice
heaven-seeming!
Into your deep teeming
may all someday rise –

Goal!
that the drift eternal
hot and cool
is driving to.

Longing
ever greater
as the womb climbs
higher above it.

Womb,
depth without end,
ever farther
as the longing lengthens.

From Pan (1916)

Joy. Woman. Humanity.
Longing that never ends
O! because the rising of humanity
is nowhere bounded.

Like a golden child
like a seashell
you came and gave your beauty.
As a golden streaming
of love's aromas
you filled the earth my dwelling.
Above, below, and on the ladder
of the All, as with the air of the earth
you filled with effervescent golden love
the dwelling of your king.
And your embraces were
the life of your veins –
out of your dream you poured yourself
on me like wind upon a tree.
Your thoughts were never elsewhere
than the eyes of your beloved.
The way the sunlight sails of itself,
swift as an arrow onto earth,
as a hind in the forest,
as a lion cub,
you were in all the showings of your love.
Like a springtime,
like a storm wind
you came into my dwelling.

From Pan (1916)

WHEN I STARE INTO YOUR EYES, BELOVED,
it is as if I roam through spaces there,
landscapes of light, no longer just
reflections, just the sun. No, my Love,

a light comes on me there, my Love,
and by my side, too gently to be named, there wells
as from a depth, as from a streaming clear
and warm and dark, a light of love.

As a man seated before the woman he loves
feels no longer warm or cold
but rises endlessly into her eyes –
so Pan rose up into her dome of beauty
through her eyes
and he was blinded
by the golden warmth of heaven
the way the Lover by his Lady
loses feeling for himself, forgets
all things, his living and his eating,
save her alone whom he now lives and eats –
so Pan was swept away into the glorious watering
hot gold of eyes,
thinking: 'If only earlier I had known
this golden consciousness; it is the end
of Nature. O, to have sweet in the head
as ripest of all fruits
a conscious image –
in the goldness of the all of All
humanity within its endless shore –
they are the sovereigns in spirit
of all the dwellings in the world of dust...'

From Pan (1916)

AND WHILE AFAR THE LIGHTNING STILL FLASHED, A BATH
began of silken streamers, a dark-beaded treasure
of silent raindrops, sprinkling
finely at first as if a scent of fennel, then
heavier, diamonds, then still
heavier, rain on every side. Finally
very heavy, one great bath
among the trees and on their wealth of flowers.
And sweet clouds arose, of aromas
and here and there the wind opened a window
on quiet. And the dark cloud
of rain that would have dwelt among the treetops
softened its streaming, and a red gleam
of anemone and sweet william could faintly
be seen, as a tiny bloom of amaranth,
a seashell on the tender edge of dark.
And down-like as the sleep that wraps sweet dreams
it rained among the high-up trees
and farther, over the silver-colored lands
visible against the walls of oak-tree trunks.
And a music, tender as if of silver
tender to the touch, and shivers of light
were made by the silver spatters and bubbles of light.
And a music, dark as from a wellspring,
was made by the dark and pliant rain
as it settled into the dark forest.

AND PAN AND THE SPIRIT WENT TO THE REALM OF LOVE
as crystalline it interwove with evening
that was clear and lucent in that kingdom.

And there, Pan and the Spirit saw a Lover,
a beautiful woman deep as a wellspring
shone through with love as is with sun
the water deep within a well,
open and clear yet secretly shone through
with love; she held love as a treasure in herself
radiant as light from in a spring,
a purple source that lighted all the Earth,
lighting all the world as one Crystal.

...

...

And the Spirit of Humanity, of the New Music
asked of her –
they stood as women, two of equal beauty –
and Pan, gazing into the Spirit's eyes
saw the beautiful maiden's form therein
and all the world behind her, earth,
so sweetly rivered in the sky's blue garden –
asked of her: 'How is it that that Sun
of Love shines stronger in your source
than ever I did see?
And why is the all of All alight

From Pan (1916)   73

with the bright crystal of your love?
And why, through your love, does Humanity
so radiate, as if its rays were nowhere bounded?'

And the maiden, like the bough blossoming in beauty
of an apple tree – she was so lit with sun –
with colors flowering straight from her source
glittering by thousands from her eyes
said clearly and yet full of feeling
deep as in the heart the soul is,
said: 'Because I love
my man as no one ever yet has loved...
For me he is the image of Humanity
whose beauty on the Earth is nowhere bounded.
For me he's the most beautiful of beauties
in the beauteous host that houses on the Earth.
Perhaps that's why the all of All's alight
with rays from me, as a single bright crystal.
Perhaps that's why Humanity's alight
with love from me, with light that's nowhere bounded.'

And Pan looked into the eyes of his Beloved,
that other lofty lady
in whom the godly lady was reflected
and thought: This is the Mystery of Love.

From *Lyrics* (1930)

Book One

The Approach of the Revolution

I.

UNTO ME CAME SHINING
a Lady in the all of All –
precious as crystal,
image of a new Humankind.

And in my heart deep love for her began,
and I began to dance with her
amidst the deeply shining all of All,
and she became my highest Love.

And in my heart deep love for her began,
and I began to dance with her
through the depths and heights of the shining all of All,
and she became my only Love.

Sweet the unseen sound of distant strings
of light, dream-like glancings –
and while we're dancing
under us we see our limbs as One.

Your bosom and that gentle something
streaming down and over you –
is it Love? an almost nothing
dreaming you from everywhere,

and the reed-like of your body, gowned
in waving dancing, up and down –
that's the only thing
that dances:
for me, it is that dance
and music – nothing else exists.

And in a wistful singleness
of joy in dancing motion
the spirits, sensing happiness
so near, join in devotion.

Dance is love's portal. Dance is holy.
Dancing is tender adoring.
To dance with you, so safely gliding –
every sense at peace, in you abiding.

Love, star in the night –
shine my heart through
that the thwart-shadowed world
be lighted too.

It's winter
far above the earth,
ice clearing,
stars like cinders.
It's lonely but a music's here.
O lonely music, be my guide:
beauty, let your wing not veer
but lead me farther, wider.

Love, star in the night –
shine my heart through
that the thwart-shadowed world
be lighted too.

The sea is lilywhite,
the sea is lilygreen,
bluegreen is her mirroring,
every sound her whispering.

In the sun
mirrored in the sea,
in the source
swinging in the moon,
in the dawn
in the dark
what I see is you,
you.

See how she's there
in her tender limbs,
in stillness, see:
beholding her beauty.

Selected Poems

I stood close by your womb,
my head nearby your bosom,
and your knee was there, full blossom
of your tenderness.

You don't know what to me
your breath, your lips are:
as if through darkness
dawn found a way.

When I think of love
it's love I love.
And it's love for you, my Love,
that lifts me into love.

II.

Never leave me, Love,
you are all I have.
You are the flood;
I am the ebb.

Nights, Beloved, I hold fast
your image with my eyes
as the seaman holds the mast
lest he go under.
But then it is I do go under, Love,
with your image in the dark of love.

That you should love me
could not be.
But you to me are lief,
believe – o nothing but believe!

After the deepest love
the heart is weak,
hardly believing,
truly dying in the Beloved.

Let me approach you tenderly,
beautiful spirit of new Music,
as my Father and my Mother,
having nothing but you only.

Gently you commence again, to dance
with me, gentle as Mother,
Spirit of Music –
the all of All's bright light
from you arising
while I'm dying
in your shadow of delight.

And the all of All becomes for me one Beauty.
Dying in it I live: within Your Beauty.

And the all of All becomes one Light around me.
I hover, still before your countenance.

Beloved! a bright dance
here: light of step
in March light still sparse
by the many-colored ponds
with each other enarmed
in the colors, warm,
purple, green,
bursting with sheen

that we're together in:
naked flames twin.

Beloved, great is the dance
far, far from the earth –
far beyond the Shore
of Stars, beyond the stellar barrier.

Love, it's a deep
dance together through the night
meshed in each other –
dance from which neither
awakens: light
as of death holds us tight.

When you dance, it's a rose
dancing, a greeny shrub of red roses:
joyful dance is what they chose!
You dance in breathings, scents and blushes all
your own – that your tossing hair
in wizardry arisen is
the fairest blossom over.

All the rest fades
where you dance into day.

Your soft-blushing head
in its hair-tangled toss
is the bud of a rose
peeping from moss.

Wondrous beauty, a girl
is dancing, keeping her robe of blue
above the ground of the earth,
thinking a song: it's new,
her mouth dreaming
in the blue of the heavenly.
She dances by beauty's shore,
deep before her
billows cloud by cloud
out of the all around about her knees
booming surf, gentle hem –
upon her breast
it rests, a blossom
never before in sight,
a peach-red bloom, her lineaments
above it lightfulfilled.
Without a thought
she dances by beauty's shore
guileless
lost to herself
in light, the
source
of the sun.
She's going, o!
Lost
in the source
of the sun.

Unveiled
she nears
and all else disappears
fading before her appearance
veined through with silence
in the air
naked.

III.

Her oval head
as the fruit,
her eyes sending
song to the beloved,
her bosom
an arching blossom,
love-wafting,
her feet tender,
the bride
pokes them into night
and waits.

Her eyes appear
as flames. We speak
in what so softly warms:
her arms.

Beloved!
Heavenly high
star, someday I
will be one ray of you. In flames of kisses
rising with you: a single shine
of beauty and of light.
Over all the earth
alight with love,
with you astir
unto eternity.

A calling comes from seaward, soft, unworded,
as if she's come. Or if I'll come to her.

As if an endless longing blows
along the dunes – gleaming gold
along the dunes.

Far Bride,
gentle beauty Bride –
out of infinity
your face pearls
through this world.

Pearling in your eye
is all the world –
every figure, every tint.
Sky. Sea. Spirit.

Goal!
that the drift eternal
hot and cool
is driving to.

Longing –
ever greater
as the womb climbs
higher above it.

Womb,
depth without end,
ever farther
as the longing lengthens.

Deep in your body I am,
in your soul: measureless
mansion.

Glorious body,
endless soul
surrounding me
perfectly.

Gone into you
and with you one
in highest blessedness,
for a moment the heart returns
upon itself its gaze.

But you are whole.
Your majesty
illumines all.
In you I be.

Her eyes
sending light.

To rise, becoming part
of her high happiness...
Music
beyond naming.

In her golden Light,
her golden Mind,
my mind.

A golden world
in which my mind's a pearl.

Now I am immersed
within your golden body's fathoms –
shining as a pearl
within your golden Mind my mind.

The inner you
is now the outer me.

IV.

The inner you
is now the outer me.

Like a lake
in which a star
is shining,
gently, from afar.

Like the glance
of a star
on a lake:
her dance.

Blackbird:
pearl
cloaked
in daybreak.

Pearl
of grace,
of love –
Beloved!

High in you,
deep in you.
Around me is no day or night.
Around me is a single light.

A single light! You around me, I'm in you,
Spirit of the Future Music.
It's out of the All, out of Humanity you now descend:
the widest wings.
You surround me, I'm in you.

You are beauty. Gazing within you,
successor to myself, I see –
you, beauty moving, living
in what's now in being.
You are in me, I am in you.
Spirit of Music! I am in you,
you've opened you for me.

It is not true that this is sunlight.
This is you.
This is not the wind that blues
across the water:
that is not so gentle:
this is you.
This is not the earth and not the heavens –
so beautiful they're not.
This is you.

O blossoming sunlight,
blossoming water!
Unending thirst
that's love's flowering!
To the showering sound
of white sourcelight
my Love lies
on my breast.

It's when I peer
into your eyes, my Love,
I see the mystery clear
that's Love.

Won over!
Love's sun
striding bright before me –
won over!
Love's source
guiding me along her crystal course.

It's said the absolute of Love's
a super-human quandary –
and yet my love for you, Spirit
of Music, knows no boundary.

Book Two

The Coming of the Revolution

I.

LIGHT OF THE ALL OF ALL!
Once you came here living,
seeking, quivering,
tall and slender skimming,
pearl of crystal,
out of all unknowing
to the shore dividing
knowing
and unknown.

And you lived, swaying
whichever way the inner would,
beauty-feathered reed, bending
into every wind.
Beautifully high, inclined
to Love!
Inclined to love,
to love as crystal!
Beloved!

From Lyrics (1930)

And now you slowly
come to know,
through strife,
yourself the Light of the all of All!
Softly shine your crystal eyes
in which are all the brightnesses
of water and of light:
the way to your heart
a valley,
a woe of clarity.

Someday you'll be one
with the all of All,
your golden limbs extending
through the knowledges
of all the shores...

O endless golden
spirit radiant,
Humanity,
it's you we love.

Rejoice on earth! Rejoice!
Faces grown blessed,
mouths turned toward heaven
for Love is found.

II.

Over the white ice
in the sun's golden shine
between the green of trees,
over that dark spring,
gliding through that palace
is the Music of Dreams.

Over the white ice
in the sun's golden shine
between the green of trees,
gliding through that unseen
palace is the Source of Dreams:
the Music.

Silent we stand, two gulls
on the ice –
around us nothing stirring:
centuries:
the palace of the world.

Pride!
Up from the source
through fire
to the sun.

A snowy hill
white as a gull
bold in the blue
and the pure gold.

A snowy hill
white as a gull
dizzily bright
with sparkling light.

The sea one blue meadow,
grassless, greenpale,
and one white wave – a flowering
in wideness without end.

Close by the sea
in the high dunes
a stream arises –
gentle is that tract,
gently slanting,
full of flower is that clime.

I see you from afar,
Beloved,
image writ in stars
of naught but love.

Like a bird
through the pearling light
I soar through the height,
the light of the world.

Great the white gull goes
in freedom bred,
wings fine as snow
in wideness spread.

White as snow
a gull goes
flying where the sea
and the blue cease.

As the dove
soars in the light –
so I soar in the light
of love.

Even the tiniest crystal,
stuff that All's built of –
tiniest atom, seems
by light of beauty, love's dream.

In the blue water
a strand of silver sand:
on this blond coast
the gulls come to rest.

Border
of sea, blue land
with no end,
never enhemmed,
source beshone
by stars alone.

Over the wave-rich sea
goes the lonesome wind
till he can find
another kingdom, wider, new, free.

Unveiled
she nears
and all else disappears
fading before her appearance
veined through with silence
in the air
naked.

You near,
veined through with silence
now, Beloved
in clouds of fire and blood...
all one love.

O Golden Spirit
of freedom –
now I'm thrusting higher,
thrusting into ever brighter, whiter, golder
Joy,
into your golden body.

III.

And wordlessly I feel myself
becoming one with her – in common
that was long in coming.

Deep goes the radiance
of night and of light, translating
All into feeling –
see the way she lies in bliss, facing
above, from eyes to soles receiving
me, as after endless byways
I plunge into my goal
of Light.

The Spirit of Music
came down and lay
as a soul all of crystal
under blue day.

Like a lightcrystal feather,
a crystalline soul
here in the blue weather
of harmony, All in the All.

On her back she lay
backward gazing
into herself. Into joy.

My Beloved
as water pure
came into the fire
of love.

The glistening fount
became the sky,
the gentle sun.

In downy repose
she naked lay;
her thought climbed high
as a bloom to the sky.

Gentle as a velvet
jewel
was her gaze
of joy.

'My thoughts...
Where have they gone?
gold and white beyond all bourn,
tender, full of love, disrobed...

when love came into me
my Love
I welled
full.

But what is that in there?
What is within?
How could I know. The peace my soul is in
is all of light

and what I see
is naught but light,
naught but love,
the light is my beloved.'

Dreaming,
all her body still,
in her averted gaze the firm,
the gentle blessed moment's will.

She lay reclining,
her head resting high,
and on her eyes, unopened, glinted
endless gladness given.

The radiant Maiden
bright as if in dawning
from the deepest fount
grew golden in the light of sun.

The all-radiant
pearl of all the years
grew heaven-white and gold
with her Beloved.

The all-radiant
that the years had seen
in water, mountain, wood –
became white light of Love.

Deep into the fount
the sun finally fell.
And the fount
rose to heaven.

In my arms
the luminous fount
turned to heaven.
I saw her face swimming
with heaven all around it,
saw her spirit swimming
in heaven.

Out of the dark of earth
arises light –
the all of All suspended in the light
of love.

Book Three

The Defeat of the Revolution

I.

AND I WAS HAPPY: THAT HER ALL-WORLD TONGUE
resounded in my sweet mother tongue.

And I followed her, her little page
through golden orchards of the night and day,
thinking the new poetry
was here, immortal in her melody.

And then I saw her. She was herself the sun
of night, facing the vast expanse
of the all of All, the timeless all-plantations
shadowed fathomless in blue and far.

And at her feet, there sat the little page,
guard of the highest pride of all the stars
blue and white-sparked, low on the horizon.
And far away the luring secret waved.

And she stepped forth to meet the all of All
farther than all the stars and plantations,
into the deep and blue and endless wide

with her golden, gold-echoing footfall.
She, the Spirit of the New Music, my Bride –
And I myself seemed most that shining page.

Karl, your image, stalwart, solemn,
fills all Europe with its beams of light.
You tower above the masses as above the tight
weavings of the sea a basalt column.

You raised the red flag straight and true
when it lay as a rag on a pile of dung,
waving again and shining for all to view –
you with your heart so nobly, purely strung.

You died. And why? because you were murdered
by capital. But also by the workers
who left you all alone with your attackers,

never listening to your lofty word.
Your love died only when it was forsaken
by the German workers. Your love was what they hated.

Rosa, great and noble, Lady of might
with your bright mind, your pure love
for the working class, your Beloved
to whom alone your life was plighted –

you walked as a high bright star
ahead of the working class, your Beloved
into battle – and your shining love
shone before, lone, ahead and far.

You died. And why? because you were murdered
by capital. But also by the workers
who left you all alone with your attackers,

never listening to your soaring word.
Your love died only when it was forsaken
by the German workers. Your love was what they hated.

And silently I raised my hot-wept eyes
toward her where she was now: the heights.

II.

Like a star in the night
you are, so far, so nigh.
And seeing you, I
realize my wait is endless
but you are so nigh.

Where the rain falls
the heart shrinks small.
And the thought creeps in, of asking
you, my Love, to take me in.

O that I could be in you,
o that I could nothing be,
whole in you, in you.
That they should seek me, finding nothing
but a spoor, a something
that is mine in you, in you.

I've tried to find,
hour by hour.
I could not find.
That was my fire.

My love! hungering, longing, eating
nor drinking: all-forgetting,
being in a gigantic wane
of all – except your face!

Because I am so sure
there is on earth no treasure
that can still the fullest longing,
I undertook to hunger
as my only living
and to seek, quivering.

After the day that never answers hunger
luckily there's night, the haven.
True, no better does night bring
the emptiness-abating thing
but since I'm one with night's cool,
because she's empty I forget
that I am too.

He who has the sunlight lacks the sun.
But though you were beyond my reaching forth –
at least I had the light
that comes from you, my source.

Beloved,
now, here,
truth:
I hurt,
want
to be
in you.
And in this want
I'm starving –
yet, the blessedness
that what I have
is love, for you.

The sea is dead,
the earth is dead –
because the Music's dead – the bread
of life.

At end of day
abyss is all –
hills and sea and sky
one boundless pall.

As evening falls
I stand by the abyss,
peering into All.
Nothing was, nothing is, nothing shall.

III.

A SINGLE TONE. OUT OF THE CONTINENT
behind me one note rises.
Like a fire in the night,
a fire in the darkness,
a stem of sound.

Like a new word
never before on earth heard.

And the sky took color in the East,
mirroring the colors in the West...

And the world came open!
And the sun came baptizing the globe
bathing her head in its glow
or like a mother, child in arm,
giving it the breast still warm,
seeing how it breathes. –
And my Love came walking over
from far over the ocean
where the stars and sun and moon,
the lights roam lonely...

And she hurried close to me, my Love,
loving me above all else because
it was as firstborn that I sung.
And she hurried close to me, my Mother,
my Protectress ever
to whose knees and breast I shoved.
And, my Wife, she came to me
and loved me deep and loyally
like water from a boulder sprung.

Nearing in silence, she placed
herself before my face
and in the space of all the cosmic canopy
gently began to speak to me:

'My precious poet,' so she spoke
in beauty, wisdom, glory –
'my poet, all-too tender one,
I was the Idea of the workers.
I was the Idea of the fighters.
I've died as an Idea
but a higher life's now mine.
I live now in the very workers –
live now in those wondrous seeds,
the councils of the workers.
Be one with them, one with them. Learn you
must, my Poet, tender one
anew.'

Thus she spoke, and gave her hands to mine
in pledge a while,
her eyes beneath high goldbrown hair
blue and staring
into mine, as the shepherd's do
a sheep's. And I went forth and joined, as one
star of the many, in the labor of the workers,
trying to learn the new truth that was theirs.

IV.

Gold in her own beaming stands the moon,
entering into the very light she frees,
and welcoming her, night rises vis-à-vis
entering into her with its deep blue.

There above, it's all one back-and-forth
of golden lighting in reflection showing
and the nightblue flood receiving it below –
shown for me here, deep in the earth's furrow.

But even while I stand here in this deep
there suddenly rises, standing there as crystal
in the gold of the moon and night of the all of All,

my Love, in golden helmet, yellow-robed
in night's balsam and come-and-going gold,
giving and receiving beam on beam.

Gold in her own beaming stands the moon,
entering into light by shy degrees,
while night, deep blue, rises vis-à-vis
letting its balsam into gold transmute.

There above, it's all one back-and-forth
of gold light standing still in self-reflection
and night self-plunging in blue cataract –
shown for me here, deep in the earth's furrow.

But even while I stand here in this deep,
above arises, sudden, like a crystal
in the gold of the moon and night of the all of All,

Myself, my lineaments in yellow robes,
in night's balsam and come-and-going gold,
giving and receiving beam on beam.

Selected Poems

Gold in her own beaming stands the moon,
entering into light while keeping clear,
with night in deep blue standing vis-à-vis,
transferring into her its own deep blue.

There above, it's all one back-and-forth
of gold light, in itself its own reflection,
and flood that in itself is redeflected –
shown for me here, deep in the earth's furrow.

But even while I stand here in this deep,
there suddenly rises, standing there as crystal
in the golden light and night of the all of All,

the One Humanity, in yellow robes
in night's balsam and come-and-going gold,
giving and receiving beam on beam.

And while I stand in dark earth's furrowing
I feel myself, my Love, and mankind growing
into one another, growing one with the all of All,
and in that, by that, forming one bright crystal.

Original texts used

The original Dutch texts of all poems translated in this book can be accessed free of charge via DBNL.org, the website of the *Digitale Bibliotheek voor de Nederlandse Letteren* or Digital Library for Dutch Literature. The *Collected Works* (Verzamelde werken) of Herman Gorter appear on this site together with numerous other editions or texts by and about Gorter.

The poems in this book appear in Volumes 2, 5, and 6 of the eight-volume *Collected Works*. The poems from *Verses* are from Volume 2, which also contains most of the 'other short poems.' *Pan* constitutes Volume 5. Volume 6 contains *Lyrics* (Liedjes) and just a couple of the 'other short poems.' The specific volume (in Dutch: *deel*) and page number of the beginning of each poem in the printed book (and scanned document) is given in the following list. For example, **2 : 115** in the list refers to *Verzamelde werken* Deel **2**, page **115**. For this example, on DNBL.org you can search for "Herman Gorter Deel 2." The scanned original document is accessible under "Downloads." On page 115 you will find the original poem *Er was toen sneeuw op het mos*, in this book translated as: "There was snow on that moss."

Selected Poems

5 : 384   And while afar the lightning still flashed, a bath
5 : 423   And Pan and the Spirit went to the Realm of Love

From *Lyrics* (1930)

The Approach of the Revolution

6 : 13   Unto me came shining
6 : 14   And in my heart deep love for her began
6 : 14   And in my heart deep love for her began
6 : 15   Sweet the unseen sound of distant strings
6 : 16   Love, star in the night
6 : 16   It's winter
6 : 17   Love, star in the night
6 : 18   The sea is lilywhite
6 : 19   In the sun
6 : 20   See how she's there
6 : 20   I stood close by your womb
6 : 21   You don't know what to me
6 : 21   When I think of love
6 : 26   Never leave me, Love
6 : 26   Nights, Beloved, I hold fast
6 : 27   That you should love me
6 : 27   After the deepest love
6 : 28   Let me approach you tenderly
6 : 28   Gently you commence again, to dance
6 : 29   And the all of All becomes for me one Beauty
6 : 29   And the all of All becomes one Light around me
6 : 30   Beloved! a bright dance
6 : 31   Beloved, great is the dance
6 : 31   Love, it's a deep
6 : 32   When you dance, it's a rose
6 : 32   All the rest fades
6 : 33   Your soft-blushing head
6 : 34   Wondrous beauty, a girl
6 : 39   Unveiled
6 : 41   Her oval head
6 : 42   Her eyes appear
6 : 44   Beloved!
6 : 46   A calling comes from seaward, soft, unworded
6 : 46   As if an endless longing blows
6 : 47   Far Bride
6 : 47   Pearling in your eye
6 : 48   Goal!
6 : 48   Longing
6 : 49   Womb
6 : 51   Deep in your body I am
6 : 52   Glorious body
6 : 52   Gone into you
6 : 53   But you are whole
6 : 54   Her eyes
6 : 54   To rise, becoming part

The Coming of the Revolution

6 : 117   Gentle as a velvet
6 : 118   'My thoughts...
6 : 120   Dreaming
6 : 120   She lay reclining
6 : 121   The radiant Maiden
6 : 121   The all-radiant
6 : 122   The all-radiant
6 : 122   Deep into the fount
6 : 123   In my arms
6 : 131   Out of the dark of earth

The Defeat of the Revolution

6 : 142   And I was happy: that her all-world tongue
6 : 142   And I followed her, her little page
6 : 143   And then I saw her. She was herself the sun
6 : 145   Karl Liebknecht
6 : 146   Rosa Luxemburg
6 : 149   And silently I raised my hot-wept eyes
6 : 158   Like a star in the night
6 : 159   Where the rain falls
6 : 159   O that I could be in you
6 : 160   I've tried to find
6 : 161   My love! hungering, longing, eating
6 : 161   Because I am so sure
6 : 162   After the day that never answers hunger
6 : 163   He who has the sunlight lacks the sun.
6 : 164   Beloved
6 : 166   The sea is dead
6 : 166   At end of day
6 : 167   As evening falls
6 : 172   A single tone. Out of the continent
6 : 172   Like a new word
6 : 173   And the sky took color in the East
6 : 174   And the world came open!
6 : 174   Nearing in silence, she placed
6 : 176   Thus she spoke, and gave her hands to mine
6 : 179   Gold in her own beaming stands the moon
6 : 180   Gold in her own beaming stands the moon
6 : 181   Gold in her own beaming stands the moon
6 : 182   And while I stand in dark earth's furrowing

Also available from Arimei Books

May, an epic poem about youth

Volume 1 of *The Essential Gorter*

May describes the magical journey of adolescence against the background of Holland's flowery dunescapes. In brush strokes of wonder-filled impressions a stunningly unspoiled girl, May, explores the promise of springtime and the intense spiritual life of youth. However, the cycle of life always moves on, and as May matures and returns to earth, she finds it readying for summer.

When Herman Gorter published *May* (Dutch: *Mei*) in 1889, this spontaneous and vibrant epic poem was immediately recognized by his peers as a landmark of Dutch literature. Inspired in part by John Keats' *Endymion* (1818), *May* was perhaps an inevitable product of the artistically revolutionary and highly lucid spirit in The Netherlands of the 1880s. While Gorter's contemporary, Vincent van Gogh, had just completed the groundbreaking Sunflowers series of paintings, Gorter succeeded with *May* in composing his own monument of colourful and innovative power.

A gripping story... breathlessly onward through magnificent word groups... full of surprising turns of phrase. .. before you know it, you'll be reading it out loud! - Lloyd Haft

This thoughtful, lyrical translation will stir the imagination and invite consideration of what makes the heart sing, even if the joy, like May, is only temporary. The poem, though, will endure.
- Editor's Pick, BookLife